Hui Shares

DAHLIA MALAEULU

illustrations by
Darcy Solia

Mila's My Pasifika Series

Hui loves to share ...

Ko Hui e fiafia lele oi fakahoa ...

with everyone, every day!

ki hō he tino, i aho uma!

On **Aho Gafua**, Hui shares her breakfast.

I te **Aho Gafua**, e fakahoa e Hui tana meakai o te taeao.

On **Aho Lua**, Hui shares her umbrella.

I te **Aho Lua**, ko Hui e fakamalu fakatahi ma tana uō.

On **Aho Lulu**, Hui shares her toys.

I te **Aho Lulu**, ko Hui e tāfafao fakatahi ma tona uho.

On **Aho Tofi**, Hui shares her book.

I te **Aho Tofi**, ko Hui e faitau fakatahi ma tona mātua.

On **Aho Falaile,** Hui shares her blanket.

I te **Aho Falaile,** ko Hui e kafu tokalua ma tona tamana.

On **Aho Tōnai**, Hui shares her song.

I te **Aho Tōnai,** ko Hui e pepehe fakatahi ma tona kaiga.

On **Aho Hā**, the last day of the week ...

Ko te **Aho Hā**, ko te aho mulimuli o te vaiaho ...

Everyone shares something with Hui ...
because she shared something
with everyone!

Ko nā tino uma nae fakahoa ki ei ia Hui ...
nae fakahoa foki kia Hui.

Glossary

Aho Gafua **Aho Gawhua**	Monday
Aho Lua	Tuesday
Aho Lulu	Wednesday
Aho Tofi **Aho Towhi**	Thursday
Aho Falaile **Aho Whalaile**	Friday
Aho Tōnai **Aho Tōnai**	Saturday
Aho Hā	Sunday

Pronunciation Guide

Short Vowel Sounds

a	ah	as in c**u**p
e	eh	as in b**e**d
i	ee	as in **e**at
o	o	as in **o**r
u	oo	as in t**o**

Long Vowel Sounds

ā	as in f**a**r
ē	as in **e**gg
ī	as in m**ee**t
ō	as in th**ough**t
ū	as in l**oo**t

Consonants

f/wh	fa/wha	as in fah
g	nga	as in ngah
k	ka	as in hah
l	ha	as in lah
m	mo	as in moh
n	nu	as in new
p	pi	as in pee
h	he	as in heh
t	ti	as in tee
v	vi	as in vee

Mila's My Pasifika Series

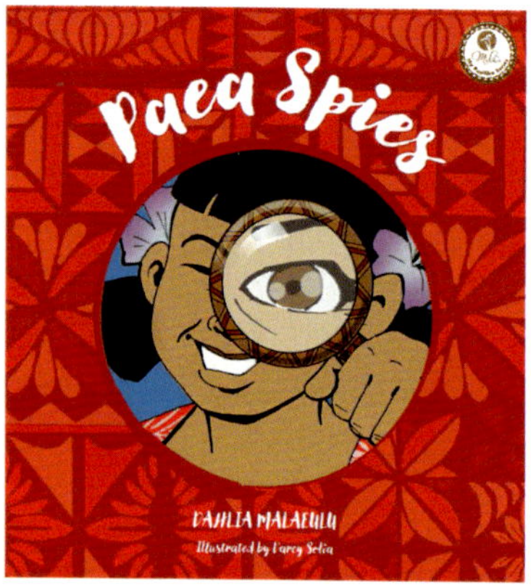

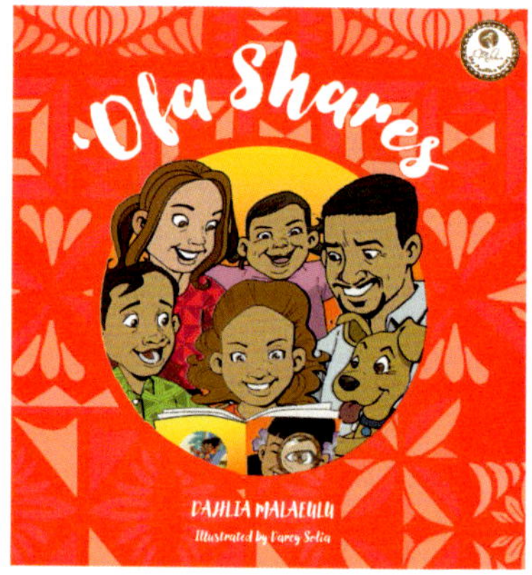

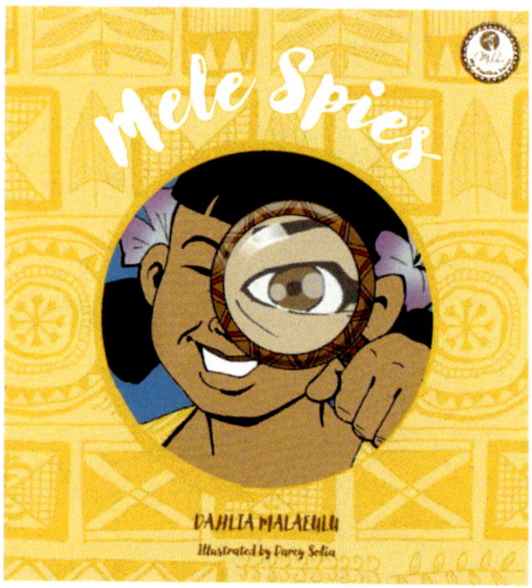

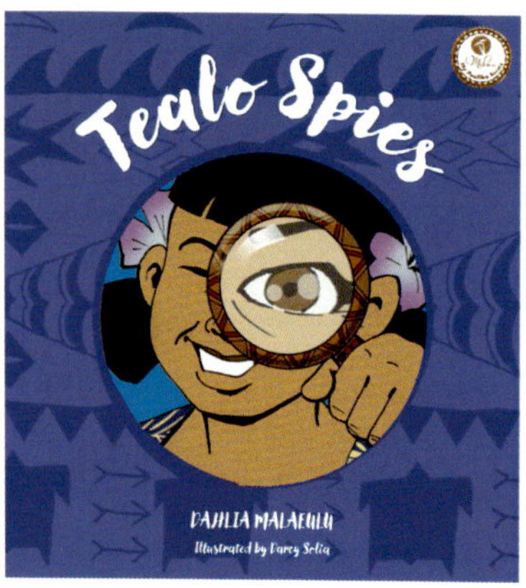

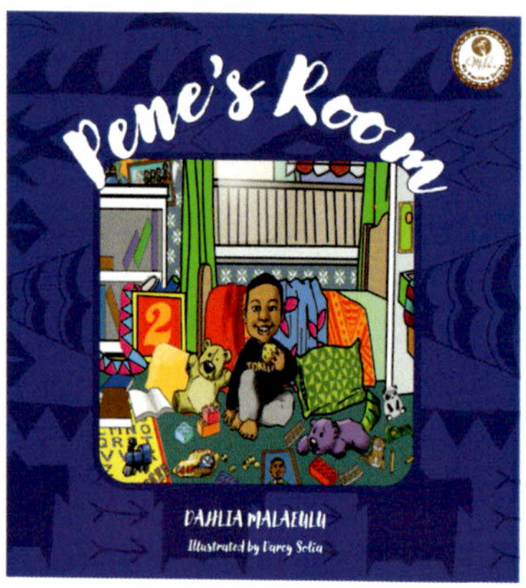

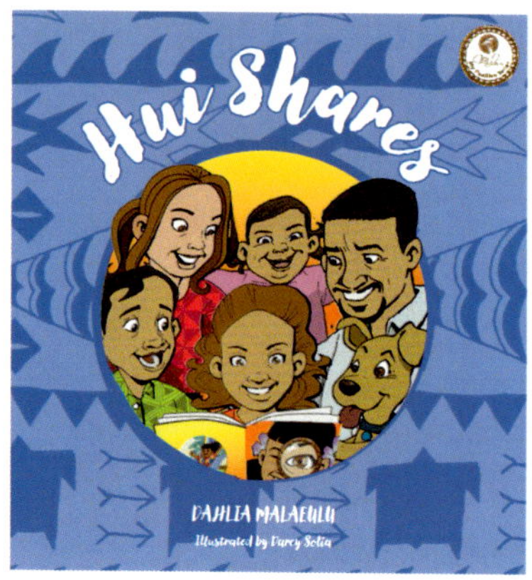

Lagi Spies
Dahlia Malaeulu

Mase's Room
Dahlia Malaeulu
Illustrated by Darcy Solia

Malia Shares
Dahlia Malaeulu
Illustrated by Darcy Solia

LOSI THE GIANT FISHERMAN
By Dahlia Malaeulu
Samoan Myths and Legends Pick a Path Collection

Fale Sāmoa
Dahlia Malaeulu
Illustrated by Darcy Solia

SIVA AFI TEINE TOA
Dahlia Malaeulu
Illustrated by Darcy Solia

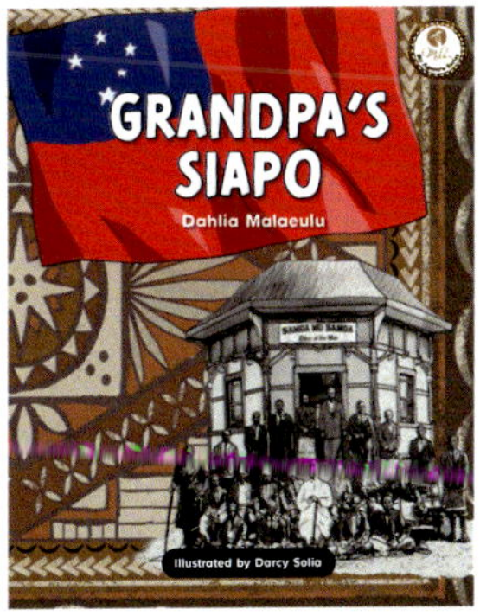
GRANDPA'S SIAPO
Dahlia Malaeulu
Illustrated by Darcy Solia

Tama Sāmoa
DAHLIA & MANI MALAEULU

DAHLIA MALAEULU
Teine Sāmoa

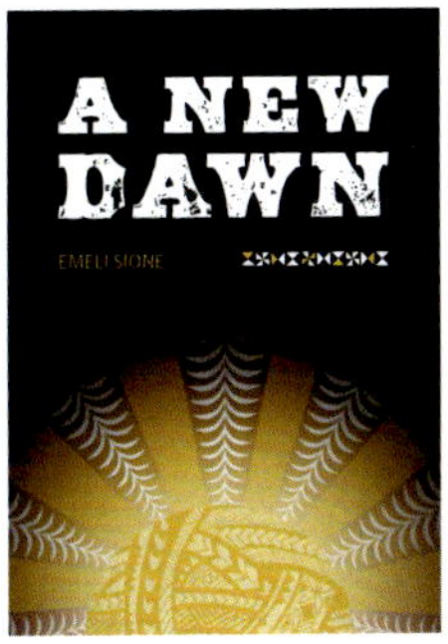
A NEW DAWN
EMELI SIONE

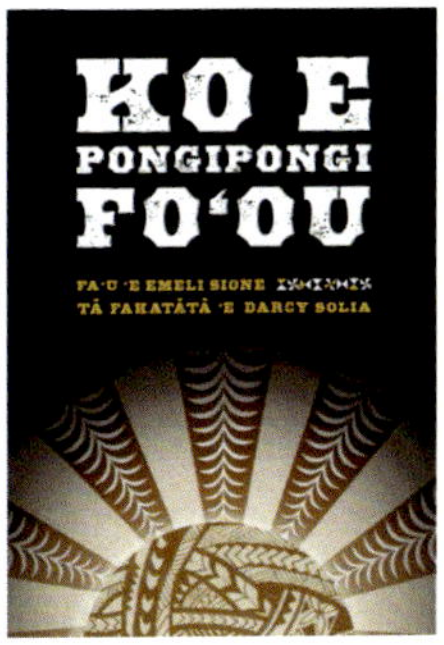
KO E PONGIPONGI FO'OU
FA'U 'E EMELI SIONE
TĀ FAKATĀTĀ 'E DARCY SOLIA

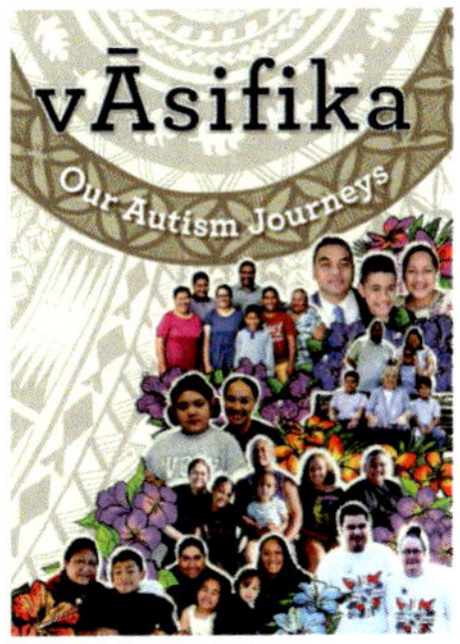
vĀsifika
Our Autism Journeys

PASIFIKA NAVIGATORS
Pasifika Student Poetry Collection

Tama Pasifika Wellbeing Journal
CONNECT
TALANOA
HEAL

Teine Pasifika Wellbeing Journal
SEEN
HEARD
VALUED

I am Pasifika Wellbeing Journal

Ko Hui e whakakoa

DAHLIA MALAEULU

Na whakaliliu e
Sale & Selina Alefosio

Na tūhia nā ata e
Darcy Solia

Ko Hui e whiawhia lele oi whakahoa ...

Hui loves to share ...

ki hō he tino, i aho uma!

with everyone, every day!

I te **Aho Gawhua**, e whakahoa e Hui tana meakai o te taeao.

On **Aho Gawhua**, Hui shares her breakfast.

I te **Aho Lua**, ko Hui e whakamalu whakatahi ma tana uō.

On **Aho Lua**, Hui shares her umbrella.

I te **Aho Lulu**, ko Hui e tāwhawhao whakatahi ma tona uho.

On **Aho Lulu**, Hui shares her toys.

I te **Aho Towhi**, ko Hui e whaitau whakatahi ma tona mātua.

On **Aho Towhi**, Hui shares her book.

I te **Aho Whalaile**, ko Hui e kawhu tokalua ma tona tamana.

On **Aho Whalaile**, Hui shares her blanket.

I te **Aho Tōnai**, e whakahoa e Hui tana pehe.

On **Aho Tōnai**, Hui shares her song.

Ko te **Aho Hā**, ko te aho mulimuli o te vaiaho ...

On **Aho Hā**, the last day of the week ...

Ko nā tino uma nae whakahoa ki ei ia Hui ...
... nae whakahoa whoki kia Hui!

Everyone shares something with Hui ...
... because she shared something with everyone!

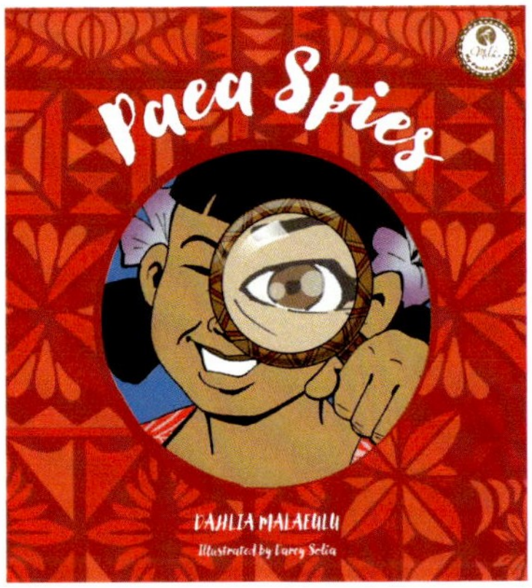
Paea Spies
DAHLIA MALAEULU
Illustrated by Darcy Solia

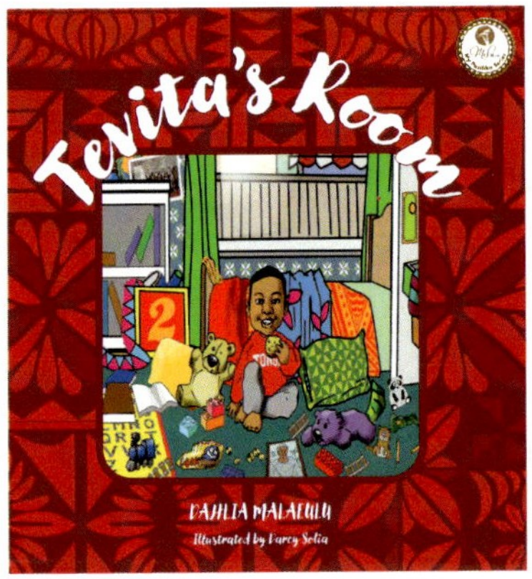
Tevita's Room
DAHLIA MALAEULU
Illustrated by Darcy Solia

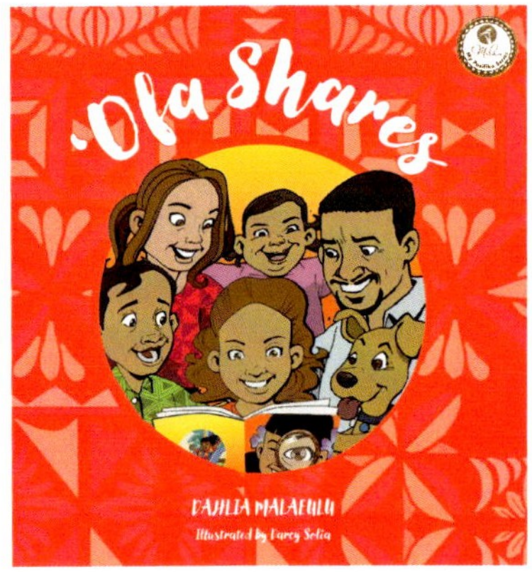
'Ofa Shares
DAHLIA MALAEULU
Illustrated by Darcy Solia

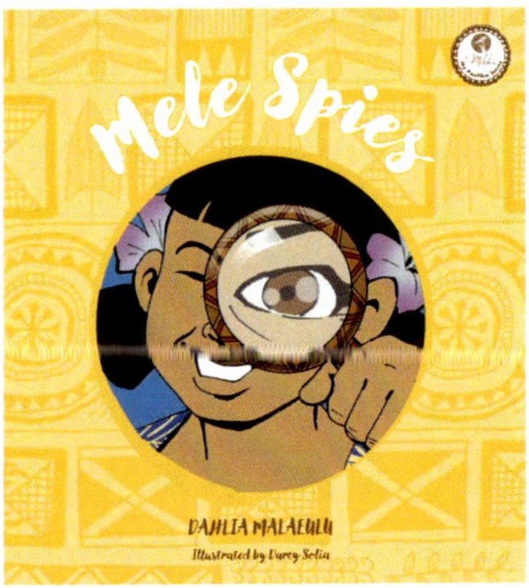
Mele Spies
DAHLIA MALAEULU
Illustrated by Darcy Solia

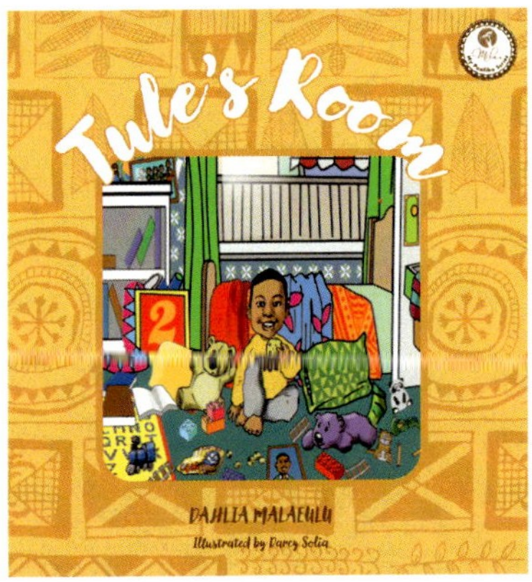
Tule's Room
DAHLIA MALAEULU
Illustrated by Darcy Solia

Moka Shares
DAHLIA MALAEULU
Illustrated by Darcy Solia

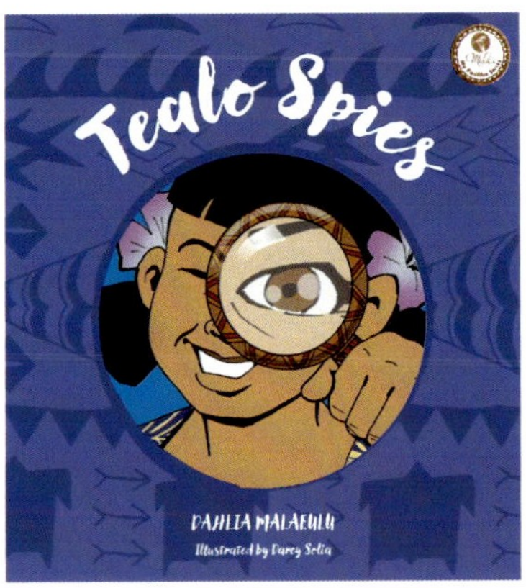
Tealo Spies
DAHLIA MALAEULU
Illustrated by Darcy Solia

Pene's Room
DAHLIA MALAEULU
Illustrated by Darcy Solia

Hui Shares
DAHLIA MALAEULU
Illustrated by Darcy Solia

Lagi Spies
Dahlia Malaeulu
Illustrated by Darcy Solia

Mase's Room
Dahlia Malaeulu
Illustrated by Darcy Solia

Malia Shares
Dahlia Malaeulu
Illustrated by Darcy Solia

LOSI THE GIANT FISHERMAN
By Dahlia Malaeulu
Samoan Myths and Legends Pick a Path Collection

Fale Sāmoa
Dahlia Malaeulu
Illustrated by Darcy Solia

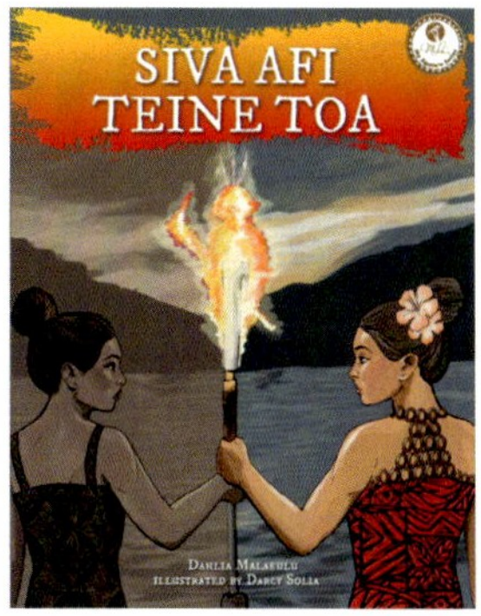
SIVA AFI TEINE TOA
Dahlia Malaeulu
Illustrated by Darcy Solia

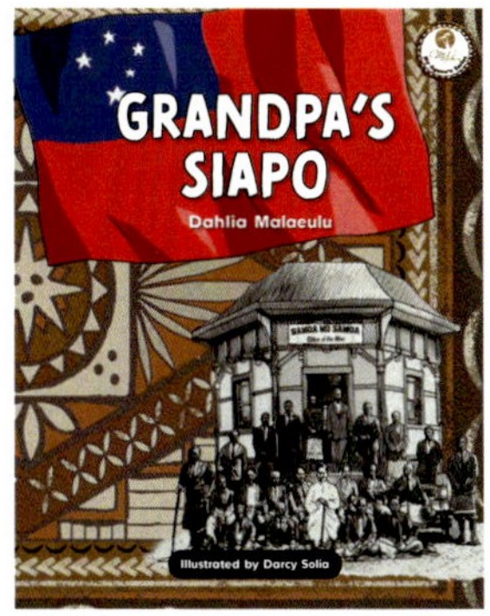
GRANDPA'S SIAPO
Dahlia Malaeulu
Illustrated by Darcy Solia

Tama Sāmoa
DAHLIA & MANI MALAEULU

DAHLIA MALAEULU
Teine Sāmoa

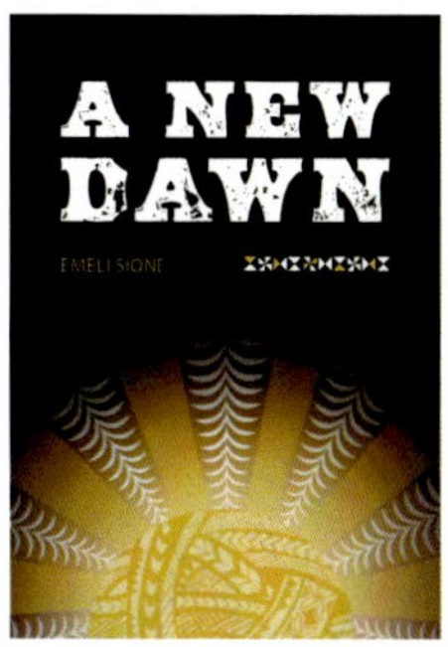
A NEW DAWN
EMELI SIONE

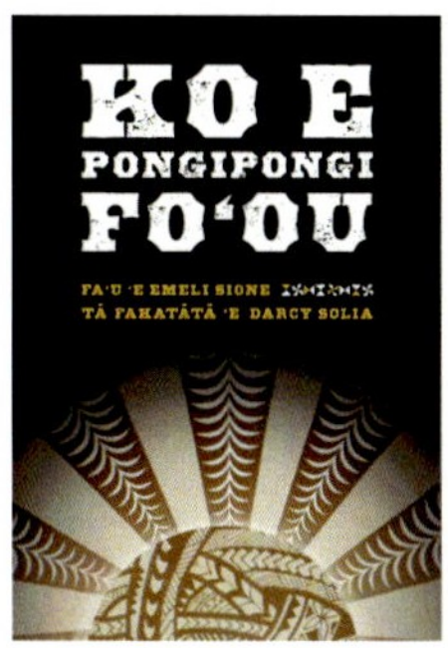
KO E PONGIPONGI FO'OU
FA'U 'E EMELI SIONE
TĀ FAKATĀTĀ 'E DARCY SOLIA

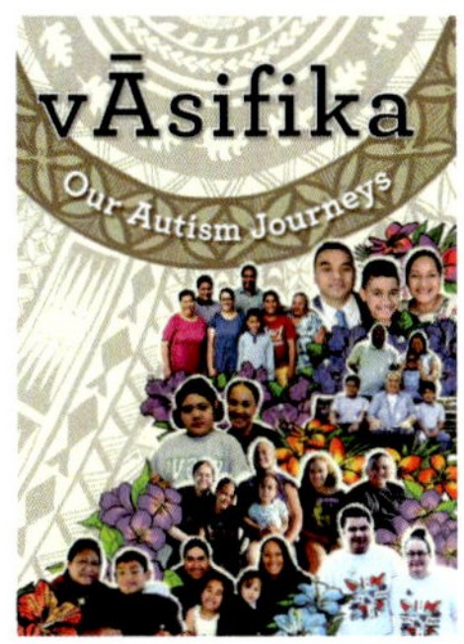
vĀsifika
Our Autism Journeys

PASIFIKA NAVIGATORS
Pasifika Student Poetry Collection

Tama Pasifika Wellbeing Journal
CONNECT
TALANOA
HEAL

Teine Pasifika Wellbeing Journal
SEEN
HEARD
VALUED

I am Pasifika Wellbeing Journal
PASIFIKA

Na lōmia e Mila's Books
www.milasbooks.com

Ko te lolomiga whakalua tenei.

Fakafehokotaki te National Library of New Zealand mō te lihi o fakamatagala mō te tuhi tēnei.

ISBN 978 1 7386061 9 1

Na tūhia e Dahlia Malaeulu
Na fakaliliu e Sale ma Selina Alefosio
Na tūhia na ata e Darcy Solia
Na teuteūa te tuhi e Liz Tui Morris
Na hiaki e Emeli Sione

COPY RIGHT LICENSING NEW ZEALAND

Recipient of a 2022 Contestable Fund Grant
from Copyright Licensing New Zealand

Published by Mila's Books
www.milabooks.com

A catalogue record for this book is available from the National Library of New Zealand.

ISBN 978 1 7386061 9 1

Original story written by Dahlia Malaeulu
Translated by Sale and Selina Alefosio
Illustrated by Darcy Solia
Designed by Liz Tui Morris
Edited by Emeli Sione

COPY RIGHT LICENSING NEW ZEALAND

Recipient of a 2022 Contestable Fund Grant
from Copyright Licensing New Zealand